A Handful of

Flowers

A Handful of *Flowers*

cookie lee

RYLAND
PETERS
& SMALL

LONDON NEW YORK

Senior designer Sally Powell

Editor Miriam Hyslop

Location and picture manager Kate Brunt

Picture research Sarah Hepworth,
   Emily Westlake

Production Meryl Silbert

Art director Gabriella Le Grazie

Publishing director Alison Starling

First published in the United
Kingdom in 2002
by Ryland Peters & Small
Kirkman House
12–14 Whitfield Street
London W1T 2RP
www.rylandpeters.com

10 9 8 7 6 5 4 3 2

ISBN 1 84172 258 8

A CIP record for this book is available
from the British Library.
Printed and bound in China

contents

introduction

There is something very special about receiving a bunch of flowers. Nature's ability to create something so delicate, fragrant and richly textured makes the gift of flowers simply priceless.

Associating a particular meaning with a flower has a long history, drawing on mythology and folklore from around the world. The Language of Flowers was popularised in Britain and North America in the Victorian era – and **A Handful of Flowers** explores and celebrates this tradition.

The book is divided into thematic chapters that reflect the key events in life – Friendship, Love & Passion, Marriage, Sadness & Loss, Health & Healing and so on. Each chapter presents a selection of flowers and other

plants with their traditional meanings, enabling you to put together a bouquet that speaks volumes.

Flowers are **always** a welcome gift. For centuries they have been part of the celebrations and rituals of life – birthdays, weddings and other religious ceremonies. But you can also brighten an ordinary day with a carefully selected bunch of flowers – by reminding a friend how much you value their kindness, or as form of congratulation for something achieved (however small). Much of this book is devoted to flowers as the messengers of love, and it is the wonderful sensuality of flowers – the velvet softness of a deep red rose, the heady fragrance of a pure white lily – that make them so appropriate for this role.

Let the flowers do the talking with **A Handful of Flowers**!

Crown Imperial *Power*

Lost for words? Send messages of hope, peace or sincerity with the Language of Flowers.

Humanity & Life

Anemone *Anemone – expectation*

Aster, White *Aster – afterthought*

Betony *Stachys officinalis – surprise*

Broom *Cytisus – humility*

Chervil *Anthriscus cerefolium – sincerity*

Chicory *Cichorium – frugality*

Chrysanthemum, White *Chrysanthemum – truth*

Cowslip *Primula veris – pensiveness*

Crown Imperial *Fritillaria imperialis – power*

Cyclamen *Cyclamen – diffidence*

Fuchsia *Fuchsia – taste*

Gentian *Gentiana – integrity*

Goat's Rue *Galega – reason*

Primula
Diffidence

Passion Flower *Belief*

Hawthorn *Crataegus* – *hope*

Honesty *Lunaria* – *sincerity*

Iris *Iris* – *a message*

Magnolia *Magnolia* – *love of nature*

Maple *Acer* – *reserve*

Mimosa *Acacia* – *modesty*

Mulberry, White *Morus* – *wisdom*

Nasturtium *Tropaeolum* – *patriotism*

Oleander *Nerium oleander* – *beware*

Olive Branch *Olea europaea* – *peace*

Passion Flower *Passiflora* – *belief*

Primula *Primula* – *diffidence*

Sweet Briar *Rosa eglanteria* – *poetry*

Sycamore *Acer pseudoplatanus* – *curiosity*

Violet, Sweet *Viola* – *modesty*

Cyclamen *Diffidence*

All the world's a stage,

And all the men and women merely players.

They have their exits and their entrances,

And one man in his time plays many parts.

WILLIAM SHAKESPEARE 1564–1616

Anemone *Expectation*

All that I desire to point out is the
general principle that Life imitates
Art far more than Art imitates Life.

OSCAR WILDE 1854–1900

One shouldn't need an excuse to give flowers
to a friend or relative – an unexpected bouquet will
instantly create happiness and make an ordinary
day suddenly very special.

Happiness

Cape Jasmine *Gardenia augusta* – *ecstasy*

Crocus *Crocus* – *cheerfulness*

Crocus, Saffron *Crocus sativus* – *mirth*

Double Daisy *Bellis perennis* – *enjoyment*

Crocus *Cheerfulness*

Parsley *Festivity*

Gardenia *Gardenia* – ecstasy

Lesser Celandine *Ranunculus ficaria* – future joy

Lily of the Valley *Convallaria majalis* – return of happiness

London Pride *Saxifraga* x *urbium* – frivolity

Mugwort *Artemisia* – happiness

Myrrh *Myrrhis odorata* – gladness, mirth

Parsley *Petroselinum* – festivity

Ragged Robin *Lychnis flos-cuculi* – wit

Shamrock *Trifolium repens* – light heartedness

Sweet Sultan *Amberboa moschata* – happiness

Sweet Vernal Grass *Anthoxanthum odoratum* – poor but happy

Tickseed *Coreopsis* – always cheerful

Tiger Lily *Lilium lancifolium* – gaiety

Violet, Yellow *Viola* – rural happiness

Wood Sorrel *Oxalis acetosella* – joy

17

Do you see O my brothers and sisters?

It is not chaos or death – it is form, union,

plan – it is eternal life – it is Happiness.

WALT WHITMAN 1819–1892

Lily of the Valley

Return of Happiness

Happy the man, and happy he alone,

He, who can call to-day his own:

He who, secure within can say,

To-morrow do thy worst, for I have lived today.

JOHN DRYDEN 1631–1700

Give to me the happy mind,

That will ever seek and find

Something fair and something kind

All the wide world over.

ELIZA COOK 1818–1889

Daffodil *Regard*

Friendship is a gift to be treasured and as we journey through life we learn to cherish old friends – and delight in new ones. Express your gratitude, admiration or warm feelings for your friends by giving an extra special gift of carefully chosen flowers.

Friendship

Snowdrop *Friend in Adversity*

Agrimony *Agrimonia eupatoria* – *thankfulness, gratitude*

Amethyst violet *Browallia* – *admiration*

Arborvitae *Thuja* – *unchanging friendship*

Bellflower *Campanula* – *gratitude*

Box *Buxus* – *stoicism, constancy*

Cactus *Mammilaria* – *warmth*

Canterbury Bells *Campanula medium* – *constancy, gratitude*

Chrysanthemum, Bronze *Chrysanthemum* – *trust me*

Bellflower
Gratitude

Coriander *Coriandrum sativum* – *hidden worth*

Daffodil *Narcissus* – *regard*

Dogwood, Flowering *Cornus florida* – *durability*

Geranium, Oak-leaved *Pelargonium quercifolium* – *true friendship*

Geranium, Scarlet *Pelargonium* – *comfort*

Honesty *Lunaria* – *honesty*

Hyacinth *Hyacinthus* – *constancy*

Mallow *Malva* – *good and kind*

Oak *Quercus* – *hospitality*

Pear Tree *Pyrus communis* – *comfort*

Peppermint *Mentha* x *piperita* – *warm feelings*

Rhubarb *Rheum* x *cultorum* – *advice*

Sage *Salvia* – *esteem*

Snowdrop *Galanthus* – *a friend in adversity*

Spearmint *Mentha spicata* – *warm feelings*

Star of Bethlehem *Ornithogalum* – *guidance*

Zinnia *Zinnia* – *absent friends*

Star of Bethlehem

Guidance

Love is like the wild rose-briar;

Friendship like the holly-tree.

The holly is dark when the rose-briar blooms,

But which will bloom most constantly?

EMILY BRONTË 1818–1848

Zinnia

Absent Friends

In friendship nobody has a double.

FRIEDRICH VON SCHILLER 1759–1805

Love is blind;

friendship closes its eye.

ANON

25

A friend is a person with whom I may be sincere.

Before him I may think aloud.

RALPH WALDO EMERSON 1803–1882

Hyacinth

Constancy

Fellowship is heaven, and lack of fellowship is hell;
fellowship is life, and lack of fellowship is death;
and the deeds that ye do upon the earth, it is for
fellowship's sake that ye do them.

WILLIAM MORRIS 1834–1896

Friendship

Our friends show us what we can do,

Our enemies teach us what we must not do.

JOHANN WOLFGANG VON GOETHE 1749–1832

Everyone calls himself a friend,

but only a fool relies on it;

nothing is commoner than the name,

nothing rarer than the thing.

JEAN DE LA FONTAINE 1621–1695

I'll pu' the budding rose, when Phoebus peeps in view,

For it's like a baumy kiss o' her sweet, bonie mou;

The hyacinth's for constancy wi' its unchanging blue,

And a' to be a Posie to my ain dear May.

ROBERT BURNS 1759–1756

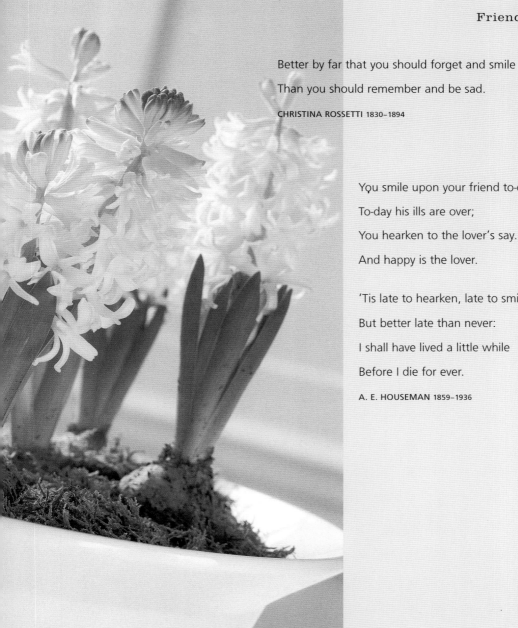

Friendship

Better by far that you should forget and smile
Than you should remember and be sad.

CHRISTINA ROSSETTI 1830–1894

You smile upon your friend to-day,
To-day his ills are over;
You hearken to the lover's say.
And happy is the lover.

'Tis late to hearken, late to smile,
But better late than never:
I shall have lived a little while
Before I die for ever.

A. E. HOUSEMAN 1859–1936

Beauty, as they say, is in the eye of the beholder and manifests itself in many forms. What better way to tell someone that they are beautiful than with nature's embodiment of perfection – a flower?

Beauty

Alyssum, Sweet *Lobularia* – *worth beyond beauty*

Amaryllis *Amaryllis* – *splendid beauty*

Cherry Blossom *Prunus* – *spiritual beauty*

Common Camellia *Camellia japonica* – *perfect loveliness*

Hibiscus *Hibiscus* – *delicate beauty*

Honeysuckle, French *Hedysarum coronarium* – *rustic beauty*

Hyacinth, White *Hyacinthus* – *unobtrusive loveliness*

Laburnum *Laburnum* – *pensive beauty*

Ranunculus – *Radiant with Charms*

Beauty

Orchid *Orchis* – *a belle*

Ranunculus *Ranunculus* – *radiant with charms*

Rose *Rosa* – *beauty*

Rose, Damask *Rosa* – *brilliant complexion*

Rose, Full-Blown *Rosa* – *you are beautiful*

Rose, Moss *Rosa* – *voluptuousness*

Stock *Matthiola* – *lasting beauty*

Variegated Tulip *Tulipa* – *beautiful eyes*

Venetian Mallow *Malva* – *delicate beauty*

Stock *Lasting Beauty*

Rose *Beauty*

Amaryllis
Splendid Beauty

See! how she leans her cheek upon her hand:

O! that I were a glove upon that hand,

That I might touch that cheek.

WILLIAM SHAKESPEARE 1564–1616

She was a phantom of delight

When first she beamed upon my sight.

WILLIAM WORDSWORTH 1770–1850

Orchid *A Belle*

For she was beautiful – her beauty made

The bright world dim, and everything beside

Seemed like the fleeting image of a shade.

PERCY BYSSHE SHELLEY 1792–1822

Was this the face that launched a thousand ships,

And burnt the topless towers of Ilium?

Sweet Helen, make me immortal with a kiss!

CHRISTOPHER MARLOWE 1564–1593

35

This is that Lady Beauty, in whose praise

Thy voice and hand shake still, – long known to thee

By flying hair and fluttering hem, – the beat

Following her daily of thy heart and feet,

How passionately and irretrievably,

In what fond flight, how many ways and days!

GABRIEL ROSSETTI 1828–1882

Shall I compare thee to a summer's day?

Thou art more lovely and more temperate.

Rough winds do shake the darling buds of May,

And summer's lease hath all too short a date.

WILLIAM SHAKESPEARE 1564–1616

Ask me no more where Jove bestows,

When June is past, the fading rose;

For in your beauty's orient deep

Those flowers, as in their causes, sleep.

THOMAS CAREW c.1595–1640

She walks in beauty, like the night

Of cloudless climes and starry skies;

And all that's best of dark and bright

Meet in her aspect and her eyes.

LORD BYRON 1788–1824

Purple Pansy *You Occupy My Thoughts*

Love
& Passion

It's not just red roses that show you love someone – there is a multitude of flowers that can express that special romantic sentiment.

Althea *Alcea rosea* – *consumed by love*

Arbutus, Trailing *Epigaea repens* – *rumours of love*

Azalea *Rhododendron* – *romance*

Beech *Fagus* – *lovers' tryst*

Blue Bottle or Cornflower *Centaurea cyanus* – *delicacy*

Busy Lizzie *Impatiens* – *impatience*

Carnation *Dianthus* – *pure and deep love*

Cedar Sprig *Cedrus* – *constancy in love*

Chrysanthemum, Red *Chrysanthemum* – *in love*

Columbine, Red *Aquilegia* – *anxious and trembling*

Cranberry *Vaccinium macrocarpon* – *cure for heartache*

Cuckoo Flower *Cardamine pratensis* – *ardour*

Dandelion *Taraxacum* – *lover's oracle*

Daylily *Hemerocallis* – *coquetry*

Love & Passion

Dittany, White *Dictamnus albus* – *passion*

Fern – *fascination*

Fuchsia *Fuchsia* – *humble love*

Glory Flower *Clerodendrum bungei* – *glorious beauty*

Hydrangea *Hydrangea* – *heartlessness*

Jonquil *Narcissus jonquilla* – *desire*

Justicia *Justicia* – *perfection of female loveliness*

Lilac, Purple *Syringa* – *first emotions of love*

Lotus Flower *Nelumbo* – *estranged love*

Mallow, Syrian *Malva* – *consumed by love*

Marigold, French *Tagetes patula* – *jealousy*

Milkweed *Asclepias* – *heartache cure*

Motherwort *Leonurus cardiaca* – *secret love*

Myrtle *Myrtus* – *love*

Pansy, Purple *Viola* x *wittrockiana* – *you occupy my thoughts*

Scabious *Unfortunate Love*

Tuberose *Dangerous Pleasures*

Beech
Lover's Tryst

Fern *Fascination*

Peruvian Heliotrope *Heliotropium arborescens* – *infatuation, adoration*

Pink *Dianthus* – *woman's love*

Scabious *Scabiosa* – *unfortunate love*

Single Pink *Dianthus* – *pure love*

Spanish Jasmine *Jasminum grandiflorum* – *sensuality*

Rose *Rosa* – *love*

Rose, Blush *Rosa* – *if you love me, you will find it out*

Rose, Cabbage *Rosa* – *ambassador of love*

Rose, Full White *Rosa* – *I am worthy of you*

Rose, Red *Rosa* – *I love you*

Rose, Yellow *Rosa* – *jealousy*

Tuberose *Polyanthus tuberose* – *dangerous pleasures*

Love & Passion

The fountains mingle with the river

And the rivers with the Ocean,

The winds of Heaven mix for ever

With a sweet emotion;

Nothing in the world is single;

All things by a law divine

In one spirit meet and mingle.

Why not I with thine? –

See the mountains kiss high Heaven

And the waves clasp one another;

No sister-flower would be forgiven

If it disdained its brother;

And the sunlight clasps the earth

And the moonbeams kiss the sea:

What is all this sweet work worth

If thou kiss not me?

PERCY BYSSHE SHELLEY 1792–1822

Had I as many hearts as hairs,

As many lives as lovers' fears,

As many lives as years have hours,

They all and only should be yours!

ANON, 17th century

Lilac

First Emotions of Love

O were my Love yon Lilac fair,

Wi' purple blossoms to the Spring,

And I, a bird to shelter there,

When wearied on my little wing!

ROBERT BURNS 1759–1796

45

Love seeketh not itself to please
Nor for itself hath any care,
But for another gives its ease,
And builds a Heaven in Hell's
  despair.

WILLIAM BLAKE 1757–1827

Hydrangea
Heartlessness

Heaven has no rage, like love to hatred turned,

Nor hell a fury, like a woman scorned.

WILLIAM CONGREVE 1670–1729

Of all pains, the greatest pain

Is to love, and love in vain.

GEORGE GRANVILLE, LORD LANSDOWNE 1666–1735

If love were what the rose is,

And I were like the leaf,

Our lives would grow together

In sad or singing weather,

Blown fields or flowerful closes,

Green pleasure or grey grief;

If love were what the rose is,

And I were like the leaf.

A. C. SWINBURNE 1837–1909

Rose *Love*

I ne'er was struck before that hour

With love so sudden and so sweet,

Her face it bloomed like a sweet flower

And stole my heart away complete.

JOHN CLARKE 1793–1864

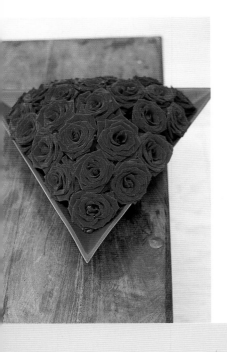

All thoughts, all passions, all delights,

Whatever stirs this mortal frame,

All are but ministers of Love,

And feed his sacred flame.

SAMUEL TAYLOR COLERIDGE 1772-1834

Red Rose

I Love You

O my luve's like a red, red rose,

That's newly sprung in June:

O my luve's like the melodie

That sweetly played in tune.

ROBERT BURNS 1759–1796

All mankind love a lover.

RALPH WALDO EMERSON 1803–1832

White Rose
I Am Worthy of You

In this give-and-take of glances,

Kisses sweet as honey dews,

When we played with equal chances,

Did you win, or did I lose?

MATHILDE BLIND 1841–1896

Not tonight, Josephine.

NAPOLEON I 1769–1821

Many waters cannot quench love,

neither can the floods drown it.

SONG OF SOLOMON 8:7, THE BIBLE

Lime Tree *Matrimony*

Flowers have long been associated with the marriage ceremony. During the years of marriage giving flowers will evoke that magical day.

Marriage

Carnation *Woman's Love*

Black Bryony *Tamus communis* – *be my support*

Carnation *Dianthus* – *woman's love*

Clover, White *Trifolium* – *I promise*

Dahlia *Dahlia* – *forever thine*

Damson Tree *Prunus domestica* – *faithful until death*

Geranium, Ivy *Pelargonium peltatum* – *bridal favour*

Geranium, Oak-leaf *Pelargonium quercifolium* – *true friendship*

Hazel *Corylus* – *reconciliation*

Holly *Ilex* – *domestic happiness*

Honeysuckle *Lonicera* – *fidelity, the bond of love*

Honeysuckle, Monthly *Lonicera* – *domestic happiness*

Ivy *Hedera* – *matrimony*

Lavender *Lavandula* – *love and devotion*

Lemon Blossom *Citrus limon* – *fidelity in love*

Lime Tree *Tilia* – *matrimony*

Pansy
You Occupy My Thoughts

Ivy  Matrimony

Oak Sprig *Quercus* – *hospitality*

Pansy *Viola* x *wittrockiana* – *you occupy my thoughts*

Peony *Paeonia* – *happy marriage*

Phlox *Phlox* – *united hearts*

Rose, Bridal *Rosa* – *happy love*

Traveller's Joy *Clematis* – *safety*

Veronica *Veronica* – *fidelity*

57

If love is the best thing in life,

then the best part of love is the kiss.

THOMAS MANN 1875–1955

There is no greater risk, perhaps, than

matrimony, but there is nothing happier

than a happy marriage.

BENJAMIN DISRAELI 1804–1881

Dahlia *Forever Thine*

Hark! The Eden trees are stirring

Soft and solemn in your hearing!

Oak and linden, palm and fir,

Tamarisk and juniper.

ELIZABETH BARRETT BROWNING 1809–1861

Love is patient and kind; love is not jealous

  or boastful;

It is not arrogant or rude.

Love does not insist on its own way; it is

  not irritable or resentful;

It does not rejoice at wrong, but rejoices

  in the right.

Love bears all things, believes all things,

  hopes all things, endures all things.

1 CORINTHIANS, THE BIBLE

Lavender

Love and Devotion

Only our love hath no decay;

This, no tomorrow hath, nor yesterday,

Running it never runs from us away,

But truly keeps his first, last, everlasting day.

JOHN DONNE 1572–1631

61

He's more myself than I am. Whatever our souls
are made of, his and mine are the same.

EMILY BRONTË 1818–1848

Peony
Happy Marriage

Oh Happiness! our being's end and aim!

Good, pleasure, ease, content!

  Whate'er thy name:

That something still which prompts

  Th' eternal sigh,

For which we bear to love, or dare to die,

Which still so near us, yet beyond us lies,

O'er-look'd, seen double, by the fool, and wise.

ALEXANDER POPE 1688–1744

63

I sing of brooks, of blossoms, birds, and bowers:

Of April, May, of June, and July-flowers.

I sing of May-poles, Hock-carts, wassails, wakes,

Of bride-grooms, brides, and of their bridal-cakes.

ROBERT HERRICK 1591–1674

'Twas when the spousal time of May

Hangs all the hedge with bridal wreaths,

And air's so sweet the bosom gay

Gives thanks for every breath it breathes.

COVENTRY PATMORE 1823–1896

The unconditional love found within a family is unique, yet often taken for granted. Remind a relative just what they mean to you with the gift of flowers.

Family

Amaryllis *Amaryllis* – *pride*

Bindweed *Convolvulus* – *bonds*

Bittercress *Cardamine* – *paternal error*

Buttercup *Ranunculus* – *memories of childhood*

Carnation *Dianthus* – *woman's love*

Cinquefoil *Potentilla* – *beloved child, maternal affection*

Crown Imperial *Fritillaria imperialis* – *pride of birth, power*

Juniper *Protection*

Dittany of Crete *Origanum dictamnus* – *birth*

Honeysuckle *Lonicera* – *the bond of love*

Juniper *Juniperus* – *protection*

Morning Glory *Ipomoea* – *affection*

Moss – *maternal love*

Mountain Ash *Sorbus aucuparia* – *I watch over you*

Nettle *Urtica dioica* – *unity*

Peruvian Heliotrope *Heliotropium arborescens* – *devotion*

Morning Glory *Affection*

Carnation
Woman's Love

Amaryllis
Pride

Primrose, Red *Primula vulgaris* – *unpatronised merit*

Sorrel *Oxalis* – *parental affection*

Sunflower, Dwarf *Helianthus* – *adoration*

Syringa *Syringa vulgaris* – *fraternal love*

Verbena, Pink *Verbena* – *family union*

Wood Sorrel *Oxalis acetosella* – *maternal tenderness*

Dwarf Sunflowers *Adoration*

Celebrate the birthdays of your loved ones with the beautiful gift of flowers. Glory in the innocence and exuberance of youth and the wisdom and contentment that comes with age.

Youth & Age

Buttercup *Ranunculus* – *childishness*

Calla Lily *Zantedeschia* – *delicacy*

Catchfly, Red *Silene* – *youthful love*

Centaury *Centaurium* – *felicity*

Cherry Blossom *Prunus* – *spiritual beauty*

Crocus, Spring *Crocus vernus* – *youthful gladness*

White Lilac *Youth*

Cherry Blossom
Spiritual Beauty

Daisy *Innocence*

Mallow *Sweetness*

Daisy *Bellis* – *innocence*

Eschscholtzia *Eschscholtzia* – *sweetness*

Fig *Ficus carica* – *longevity*

Guelder Rose *Viburnum opulus* – *age*

Hyacinth *Hyacinthus* – *sport and play*

Larkspur, Pink *Consolida* – *lightness*

Lilac, White *Syringa* – *youth*

Lily *Lilium* – *purity and modesty*

Lily, White *Lilium* – *purity*

Mallow *Malva* – *sweetness*

Marjoram *Origanum* – *blushes*

Meadow Saffron *Colchicum autumnale* – *growing old*

Medlar *Mespilus germanica* – *mature grace*

Peony *Paeonia* – *bashfulness and diffidence*

Poplar, White *Populus alba* – *time*

Primrose *Primula vulgaris* – *early youth*

Rosebud *Rosa* – *youth*

Star of Bethlehem *Ornithogalum* – *purity*

Wild Plum Tree *Prunus americana* – *independence*

Willow *Salix* – *freedom*

73

Twenty years hence my eyes may grow

If not quite dim, yet rather so,

Still yours from others they shall know

Twenty years hence.

WALTER SAVAGE LANDOR 1775–1864

Lily *Purity* *& Modesty*

Behold her there

As I beheld her ere she knew my heart,

My first, last love: the idol of my youth,

The darling of my manhood, and alas!

Now the most blessed memory of mine age.

ALFRED, LORD TENNYSON 1809–1892

No spring, nor summer beauty hath such grace,

As I have seen in one autumnal face.

JOHN DONNE 1572–1631

How cunningly nature hides every wrinkle
of her inconceivable antiquity under rose
and violets and morning dew!

RALPH WALDO EMERSON 1803–1883

Youth & Age

Crabbed Age and Youth cannot live together:

Youth is full of pleasance, age is full of care;

Youth like summer morn, age like winter weather;

Youth like summer brave, age like winter bare:

Youth is full of sport, age's breath is short;

Youth is nimble, age is lame:

Youth is hot and bold, age is weak and cold,

Youth is wild, and age is tame.

Age, I do abhor thee; youth, I do adore thee;

O, my love, my love is young:

Age, I do defy thee, O! sweet shepherd, hie thee,

For methinks thou stay'st too long.

WILLIAM SHAKESPEARE 1564–1616

There is no despair so absolute as that which comes with the first moments of our first great sorrow, when we have not yet known what it is to have suffered and be healed, to have despaired and have recovered hope.

GEORGE ELIOT 1819–1890

I love everything that's old: old friends old times, old manners, old books, old wines.

OLIVER GOLDSMITH 1728–1774

If youth knew, if age could.

HENRI ESTIENNE 1531–1598

Tulip *Fame*

Daffodil *Egotism*

Ambition
& Success

**Support your friends and family in their dreams and
achievements. Send a bouquet of carefully chosen flowers
for good luck, courage or success.**

Buttercup *Ranunculus* – *riches*

Cardinal Flower *Lobelia cardinalis* – *distinction*

Chestnut Tree *Castanea* – *luxury*

Columbine, Purple *Aquilegia* – *resolved to win*

Ambition & Success

Coronilla *Coronilla* – *success to you*

Daffodil *Narcissus* – *egotism*

Foxglove *Digitalis* – *occupation, wish*

Heather, White *Calluna* – *good luck*

Hepatica *Hepatica* – *confidence*

Hollyhock *Alcea* – *ambition*

Kingcup *Caltha palustris* – *desire of riches*

Laurel *Prunus lusitanica* – *perseverance*

Lupine *Lupinus* – *imagination*

Mugwort *Artemisia* – *good luck*

Nemophila *Nemophila* – *success everywhere*

Orchid, Bee *Ophrys apifera* – *industry*

Osmunda *Osmunda* – *dreams*

Palm *Palm* – *victory*

Polyanthus *Primula polyantha* – *confidence*

Poplar, Black *Poplus nigra* – *courage, daring*

Service Tree *Sorbus latifolia* – *prudence*

Tulip *Tulipa* – *fame*

Buttercup *Riches*

82

Service Tree
Prudence

Success is counted sweetest
By those who ne'er succeed.
To comprehend a nectar
Requires sorest need.

EMILY DICKINSON 1830–1886

Tulip *Fame*

Even for learned men, love of fame
is the last thing to be given up.

TACITUS AD c.56–AFTER 117

When a true genius appears in the
world, you may know him by this sign,
that the dunces are all in confederacy
against him.

JONATHAN SWIFT 1667–1745

Ambition & Success

I am a parcel of vain strivings tied

  By a chance bond together,

Dangling this way and that, their links

  Were made so loose and wide,

    Methinks,

  For milder weather.

HENRY DAVID THOREAU 1817–1862

Lowliness is young Ambition's ladder,

Whereto the climber upward turns his face.

WILLIAM SHAKESPEARE 1564–1616

The bravest trophy ever man obtained

Is that which o'er himself himself hath gained.

ANON

We have short time to stay as ye,

We have as fleet a spring,

As quick a growth to meet decay

As you or anything:

We die

As your hours do, and dry

Away,

Like to the summer's rain,

Or as the pearls of morning dew,

Ne'er to be found again.

ROBERT HERRICK 1591–1674

Daffodil *Egotism*

Narcissi, the fairest of them all,

Who gaze on their eyes in the stream's recess,

Till they die of their own dear loveliness.

PERCY BYSSHE SHELLEY 1792–1822

Work is the grand core of all
the maladies and miseries that
ever beset mankind.

THOMAS CARLYLE 1795–1881

Foxglove *Occupation*

Genius does what it must, and Talent does what it can.

OWEN MEREDITH 1831–1891

Blessed is he who has found his work;

let him ask no other blessedness.

THOMAS CARLYLE 1795–1881

Coping with loss can be profoundly difficult and seemingly insurmountable. When words fail, the gift of flowers can sometimes offer a little comfort and consolation.

Sadness & Loss

Rosemary *Remembrance*

Aloe *Aloe – sorrow*

Asphodel *Asphodelus aestivus – regret*

Bay Leaf *Laurus nobilis – no change till death*

Belladonna Lily *Amaryllis belladonna – silence*

Black Poplar *Populus nigra – affliction*

Butterfly Weed *Asclepias tuberosa – let me go*

Calycanthus *Calycanthus – benevolence*

Camellia *Camellia – pity*

Cedar *Cedrus – think of me*

Clover, White *Trifolium – think of me*

Poppy
Consolation

93

Sadness & Loss

Cypress *Cupressus* – *despair, death, mourning*

Elecampane *Inula helenium* – *tears*

Globe Amaranth *Gomphrena globosa* – *immortality*

Harebell *Campanula rotundifolia* – *grief, pain*

Helenium *Helenium* – *tears*

Hemp *Cannabis sativa* – *fate*

Hyacinth *Hyacinthus* – *benevolence*

Hyacinth, Purple *Hyacinthus* – *sorrow*

Jasmine, Carolina *Gelsemium sempervirens* – *separation*

Lilac *Syringa* – *memory*

Locust *Robinia pseudoacacia* – *love beyond the grave*

Michaelmas Daisy *Aster novi-belgii* – *farewell*

Mimosa (Sensitive Plant) *Mimosa pudica* – *delicate feelings*

Pansy, Purple *Viola* x *wittrockiana* – *you occupy my thoughts*

Pansy, Yellow *Viola* x *wittrockiana* – *think of me*

Periwinkle *Vinca* – *sweet memories*

Purple Pansy
You Occupy My Thoughts

94

Scabious *Unfortunate Love*

Sweet Pea *Departure*

Pimpernel *Anagallis* – *change*

Pine, Black *Pinus nigra* – *pity*

Poppy *Papaver* – *consolation*

Poppy, White *Papaver* – *sleep of the heart*

Rose, Christmas *Helleborus niger* – *relieve my anxiety*

Rose, Sweetbriar *Rosa eglanteria* – *sympathy*

Rose, White *Rosa* – *silence*

Rosemary *Rosmarinus officinalis* – *remembrance*

Scabious, Purple *Scabiosa* – *unfortunate love*

Snowdrop *Galanthus* – *consolation*

Sweet Pea *Lathyrus odoratus* – *departure*

Virgin's Bower *Clematis* – *filial love*

Wormwood *Artemisia absinthium* – *absence*

Give me my Romeo; and, when he shall die,

Take him and cut him out in little stars,

And he will make the face of heaven so fine

That all the world will be in love with night

And pay no worship to the garish sun.

WILLIAM SHAKESPEARE 1564–1616

And all my days are trances,

And all my nightly dreams

And where thy grey eye glances,

And where thy footstep gleams –

In what ethereal dances,

By what eternal streams.

EDGAR ALLAN POE 1809–1849

Sweet Pea
Departure

Remember me when I am gone away,

Gone far away into the silent land;

When you can no more hold me by the hand,

Nor I half turn to go yet turning stay.

CHRISTINA ROSSETTI 1830–1894

97

Here are sweet peas, on tiptoe for a flight:

With wings of gentle flush o'er delicate white,

And taper fingers catching at all things,

To bind them all about with tiny rings.

JOHN KEATS 1795–1821

When my self is not with you, it is nowhere.

HÉLOISE c.1098–1164

'Tis better to have loved and lost
Than never to have loved at all.

ALFRED, LORD TENNYSON 1809–1892

Poppy

Consolation

Come to me in the silence of the night;

Come in the speaking silence of a dream;

Come with soft rounded cheeks and eyes as bright

As sunlight on a stream;

Come back in tears,

O memory, hope, love of finished years.

CHRISTINA ROSSETTI 1830–1894

The healing qualities of flowers and herbs
have been appreciated for centuries.
As a gift for an unwell friend, create
a bouquet that through scents, textures
and colours will sooth and calm.

Health
& Healing

Balm of Gilead *Cedronella canariensis* – cure, relief, healing

Bluets *Hedyotis* – content

Box *Buxus* – stoicism

Camomile *Chamaemelum nobile* – energy in adversity

Cinnamon Tree *Cinnamomum* – forgiveness of injuries

Camomile
Energy in Adversity

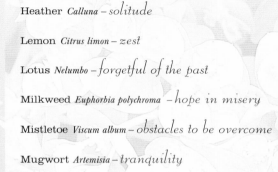

Heather *Calluna* – *solitude*

Lemon *Citrus limon* – *zest*

Lotus *Nelumbo* – *forgetful of the past*

Milkweed *Euphorbia polychroma* – *hope in misery*

Mistletoe *Viscum album* – *obstacles to be overcome*

Mugwort *Artemisia* – *tranquility*

Milkweed *Hope in Misery*

Stonecrop *Tranquility*

Oak Leaves *Quercus* – *bravery*

Periwinkle, White *Vinca* – *pleasant recollection*

Pine *Pinus* – *endurance*

Pitch Pine *Pinus rigida* – *time and faith*

Poppy, White *Papaver* – *sleep*

Stonecrop *Sedum* – *tranquility*

Heather *Solitude*

Pine *Endurance*

White Poppy *Sleep*

105

A History of
the Language of Flowers

The origins of the language of flowers can be traced back to ancient fables and myths. Flowers have been attributed with various meanings and significance for centuries around the world.

The language of flowers as we know it today is thought to have been introduced to Europe in the eighteenth century by Lady Wortley Montagu and Aubry de la Mottraye. Letters written by Lady Montagu during a visit to Turkey in 1717 spoke of the Persian 'language of objects'. This same practice of associating objects with meanings featured in de la Mottraye's account of his visit to the court of Charles XII in Turkey, published in 1727. The concept of a floral language quickly became popular throughout Europe. In 1818 Charlotte de la Tour's **Le Langage des Fleurs**, a French dictionary with over 800 meanings for flowers plants and herbs, was published. Her dictionary is thought to have been the inspiration and basis of a multitude of language of flowers books published internationally in subsequent years.

Assigning meaning to flowers became immensely popular in Britain and North America during the Victorian era, perhaps because it allowed a freedom of expression otherwise frowned upon during the time. Feelings and emotions considered taboo could be expressed with flowers.

With such a long history it is no surprise that a definitive language of flowers does not exist. Several meaning can be assigned to an individual flower or a single sentiment can be associated with more than one flower. It is the charm and romance of this tradition that makes saying it with flowers as popular today as ever.

Credits

Architects & designers whose work is featured in this book:

Ann Boyd Design Ltd.
33, Elystan Place
London, SW3 3NT
Page: 34 r

Nelly Guyot
Interior designer and photographic stylist
12, rue Marthe Edouard
92190 Meudon
France
Page: 106

Ocke Mannerfelt
Architect
Hamnvägen 8
S–18351 Täby
Sweden
Page: 104 r

Lena Proudlock
Furniture Design
Drews House
Leighterton
Tetbury
Gloucestershire, GL8 8UN
Page: 86

Enrica Stabile
L'Utile e il Dilettevole
Antiques dealer, interior decorator and stylist
Via della Spiga, 46
Milan
Italy
t. (0039) 0276 00 84 20
Page: 2

Credits

Images in this book were taken from the following Ryland Peters & Small books:

Apartment, The Colour Design Source Book, Comfortable Country, Christmas Details, Gardening Journal, A Handful of Herbs, Junk Style, Lighting, New Country Garden, Open Air Living, The Garden Plant Selector, Planted Junk, Pure Scents for Relaxation, Pure Scents for Romance, Pure Scents for Wellbeing, Pure Style, Pure Style Outside, Recycled Spaces, The Relaxed Home, Ribbons, The Seasonal Home, Simple Flowers, Table Inspirations, Vital Colour and *Wedding Details*

Credits

Photographers credits:

Front endpapers l James Merrell; front endpapers r Polly Wreford; 1 Polly Wreford; 2 Christopher Drake/Enrica Stabile's house in Brunello, Italy; 3 Tom Leighton; 4 James Merrell; 5 David Montgomery; 6–9 Steve Painter; 10–12 James Merrell; 12–13 Pia Tryde; 13 inset Jerry Harpur; 14 Sandra Lane; 14–15 David Montgomery; 15 James Merrell; 16 Jerry Harpur; 16–17 Caroline Arber; 18 l Sandra Lane; 18 r Polly Wreford ; 19 David Montgomery; 20 & 21 James Merrell; 22 & 23 inset Jerry Harpur; 23, 24 & 25 r James Merrell; 25 l Pia Tryde; 26 & 27 James Merrell; 28 Christopher Drake; 28–29 Henry Bourne; 30–33 & 34 l James Merrell; 34 r Chris Everard/Interior Designer Ann Boyd's own apartment in London; 35 Polly Wreford; 36 James Merrell; 36–37 Ray Main/Greville & Sophie Worthington's home in Yorkshire; 38 Tom Leighton; 39 Pia Tryde; 40 Polly Wreford; 41 David Montgomery; 42 & 42–43 James Merrell; 44–45 Polly Wreford/Mary Foley's house in Connecticut; 45 Polly Wreford; 46 l Sandra Lane; 46 r & 47 Polly Wreford; 48 & 48–49 James Merrell; 49 Polly Wreford; 50 l James Merrell; 50 r Tom Leighton; 51 Ray Main; 51 inset Pia Tryde; 52 & 53 Polly Wreford; 54 Christopher Drake/Josephine Ryan's house in London; 55 Francesca Yorke; 56 & 57 Sandra Lane; 58 l James Merrell; 58 r Jerry Harpur; 59 David Brittain; 60 Pia Tryde; 60–61 & 61 inset David Montgomery; 62 l Polly Wreford; 62 r Pia Tryde; 63 David Brittain; 64 Tom Leighton; 65 l Polly Wreford; 65 r David Brittain; 66–67 Pia Tryde; 67 Caroline Arber; 68, 68–69 & 69 James Merrell; 70–71 Polly Wreford; 71 James Merrell; 72 Polly Wreford; 73 Jerry Harpur; 74–76 & 76–77 James Merrell; 77 Tom Leighton; 78–79 & 79 Polly Wreford; 80–81 Henry Bourne; 81 Polly Wreford; 82 Melanie Eclare; 83 Sandra Lane; 84 & 85 James Merrell; 86 Simon Upton/Lena Proudlock's house in Gloucestershire; 86–87 Henry Bourne; 87 Pia Tryde; 88–89 & 89 Henry Bourne; 90 & 90–91 Pia Tryde; 91 Tom Leighton; 92 Caroline Arber; 93 Melanie Eclare; 94 Jerry Harpur; 95 James Merrell; 96–97 Polly Wreford; 97 Pia Tryde; 98–99 James Merrell; 100–101 Pia Tryde; 102–103 Simon Upton; 103 & 104 l Jerry Harpur; 104 r Simon Upton/A house in Sweden designed by Ocke Mannerfelt; 105 James Merrell; 105 inset Jerry Harpur; 106 Christopher Drake/Nelly Guyot's house in Ramatuelle, France, styled by Nelly Guyot; 108–109 James Merrell; 110–113 Steve Painter; back endpapers l Pia Tryde; back endpapers r James Merrell.

The author and publisher would like
to thank all those who kindly allowed
us to photograph their work or homes.